ABC Saints Coloring Book

By Nicole M. McGinnis

St. Jerome Library
WWW.STJEROMELIBRARY.ORG

Copyright ©2017, 2021 by St. Jerome Library Press

All rights reserved.

No part of this book may be reproduced or transmitted in any form or by any means, electronic or mechanical, including photocopying, recording, or by any information storage or retrieval system, without written permission from the publisher.

A is for St. Athanasius

Feast day: May 2

St. Athanasius was born in Egypt at the end of the 3rd century. He was one of God's chosen defenders of the Church during the Arian heresy. His life was constantly in danger from heretics. One time, while going down a river in a boat, in escape of an assassin ordered to kill him, the assassin came upon him. He asked, "Have you seen Athanasius?" Athanasius replied, "He is not far off. If you hurry, you will catch him." The assassin then hurriedly left him and St. Athanasius, by the grace of God, arrived safe at his destination.

St. Athanasius is regarded as one of the great doctors of the Church, steadfast and true, through all dangers.

St. Athanasius, pray for us!

A

~ 3 ~

B is for St. Boniface

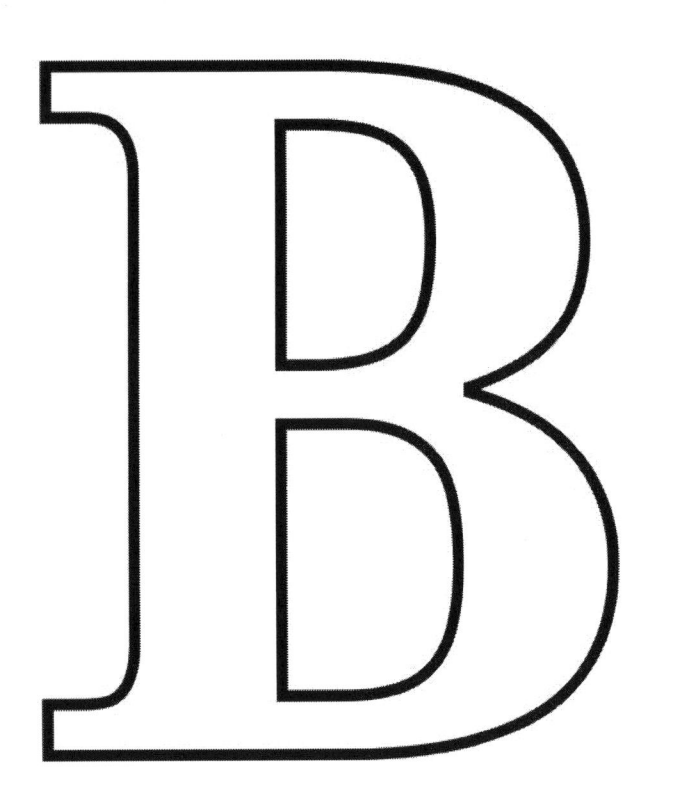

Feast day: June 5

St. Boniface was born in England in the year 680. He received the blessing of the Pope to convert those in Germany. Everywhere he went, he was in danger for his life because of his destroying pagan temples and idols. He came one day to a mighty oak which was placed in honor of the false pagan god, Jupiter. Filled with love of God, he chopped down this huge tree with an ax, and then used the very wood to build a beautiful altar for one of God's churches.

In the end, he was martyred by armed pagans, with fifty-two of his newly-baptized flock. He willingly gave up his life to God whom he loved so well.

St. Boniface, pray for us!

B

C is for St. Christina

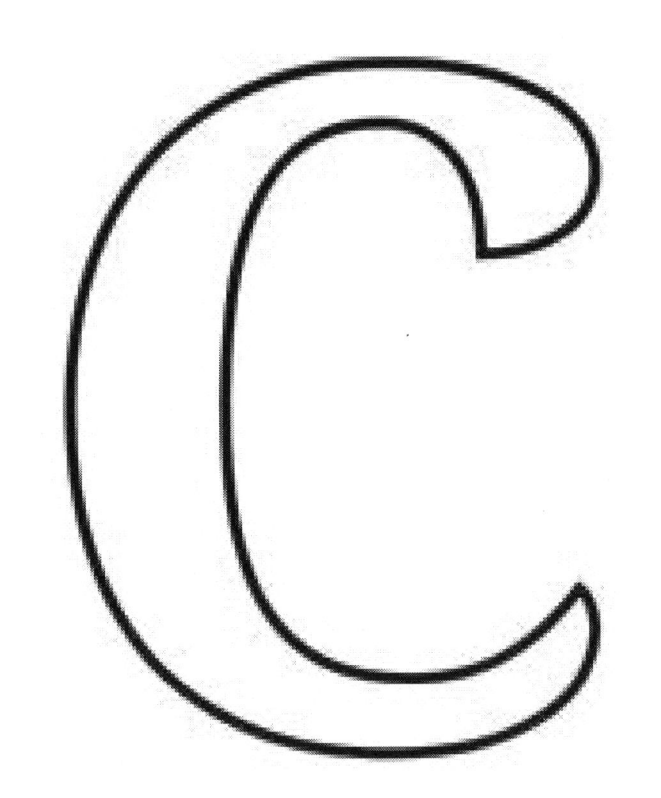

Feast day: July 24

St. Christina was born to a peasant family in 1150 AD. She died when she was just 21 years of age. Appearing before God, He asked her if she would prefer to go to heaven or return to earth for a time to offer penance and save souls. She chose to return to earth. Because of her great charity, God rewarded her with the gift of agility. She was often seen to "fly" from treetop to treetop. If one could not find Christina, it was common to look up and see her upon the roof of a house! She said that the smell of sinners was often a great burden to her. By way of sacrifice, she dressed in rags and would endure great pains by her own hand to offer as penance.

St. Christina, pray for us!

~7~

D is for St. Denis

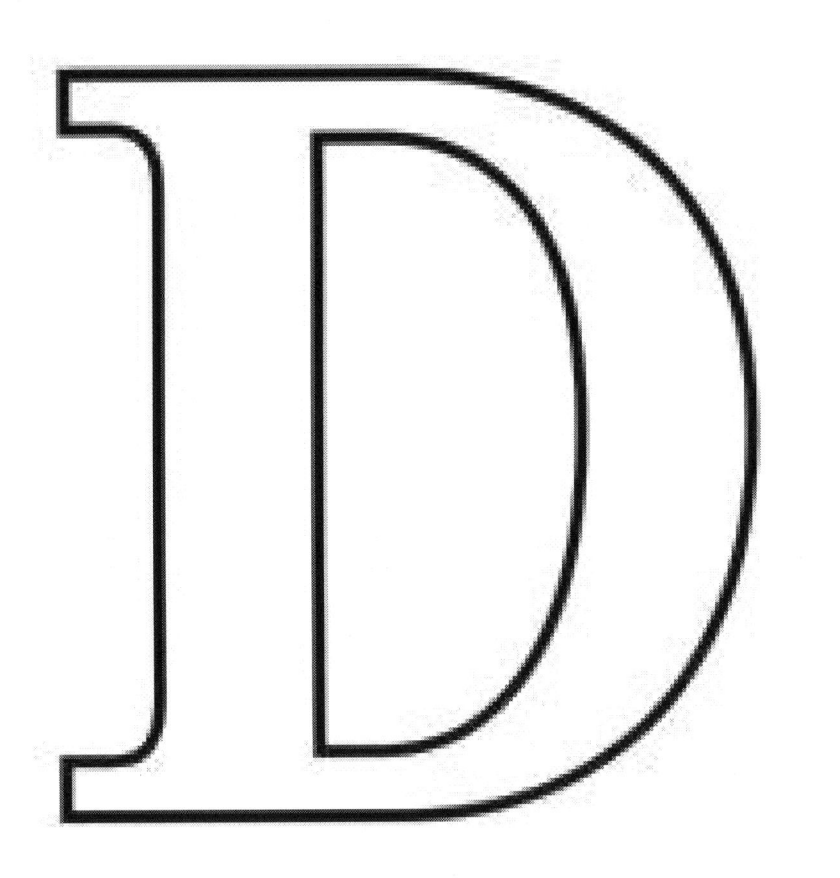

Feast day: October 9

St. Denis, also known as Dionysius, lived while Our Blessed Mother was on earth. He actually met and spoke with her! He said that if he did not already know that Our Lord was God, he would have thought Mary to be divine. He was an eloquent preacher, an excellent writer, and finally received the crown of martyrdom at the old age of 110.

After his head was cut off in one swift stroke, St. Denis' body remained alive by miraculous power, stepped over to his head, picked it up, and carried it two thousand paces, where later a church was built, in his honor!

St. Denis, pray for us!

~ 9 ~

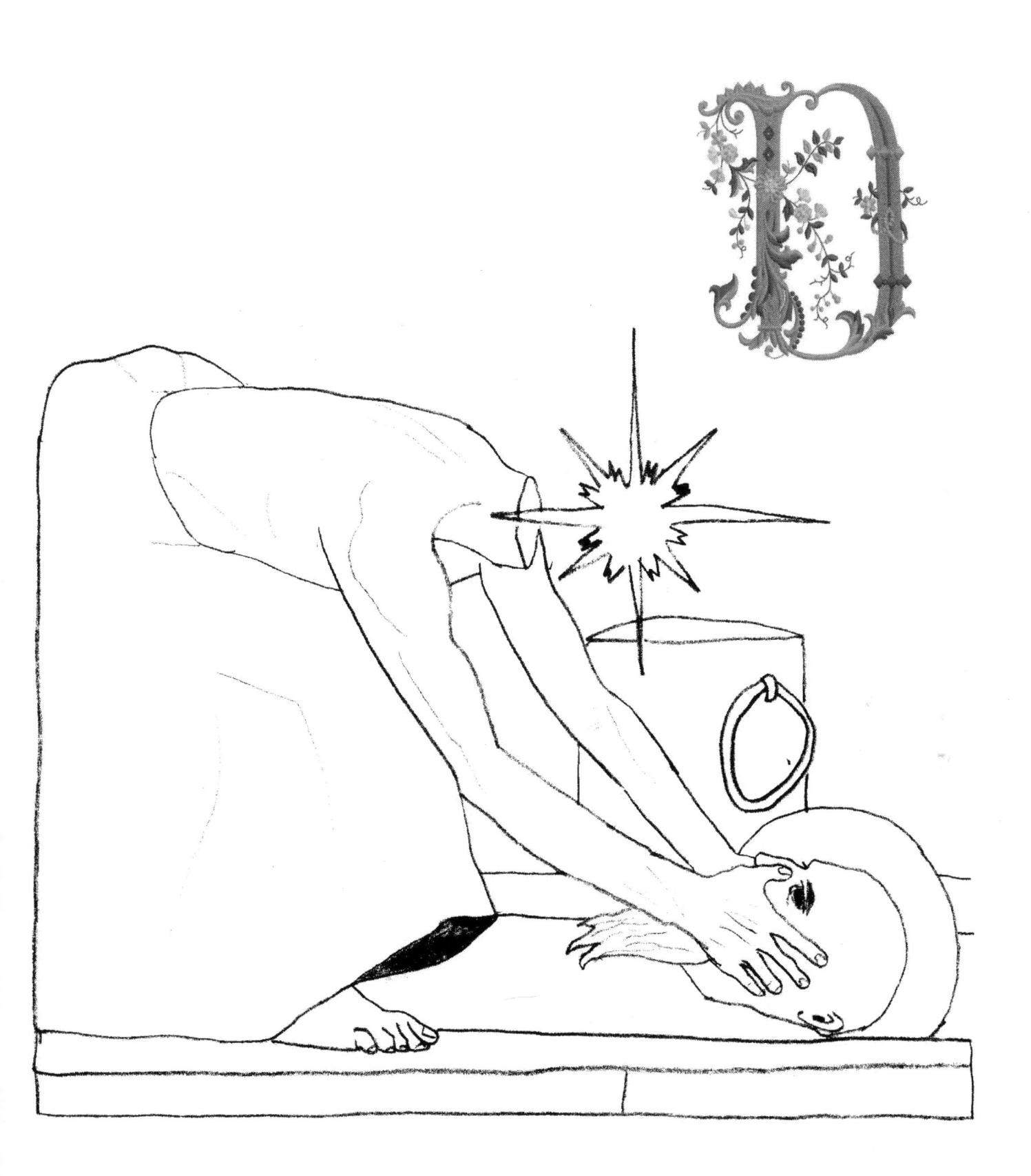

E is for St. Euphrasia

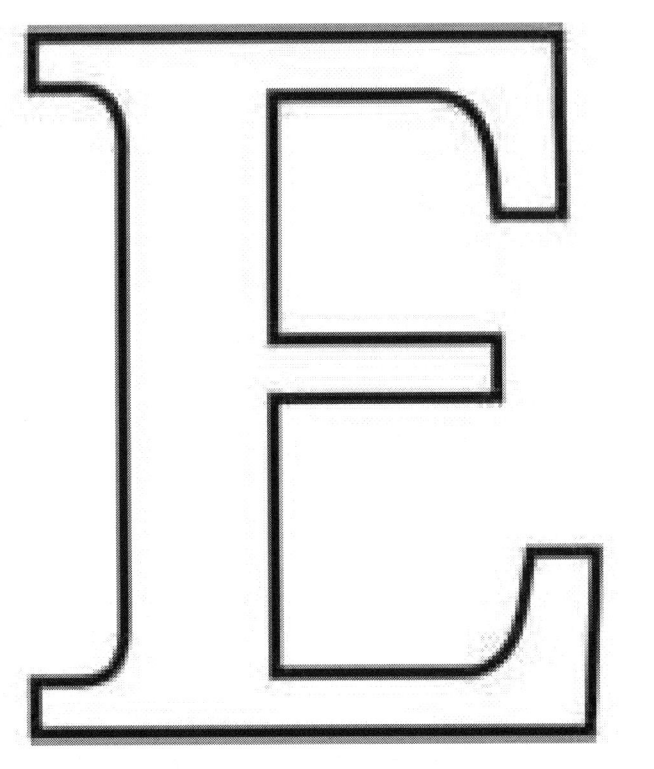

Feast day: March 13

St. Euphrasia was born in the 4th century. Her pious widowed mother was thrilled when 7-year-old Euphrasia begged to be admitted into the convent as a Religious Sister. She was a devoted and loving spouse to Our Lord. Euphrasia's wonderful abbess often would give her painful and humbling penances when Euphrasia was tempted strongly to sin. One of these penances was to carry very heavy stones from one place to another. One time, she did this labor for 30 days until the devil was finally driven away by her wonderful humility and obedience. She was also given the ability to perform miracles both before and after her death in 410 at the age of thirty.

St. Euphrasia, pray for us!

F

F is for St. Flora

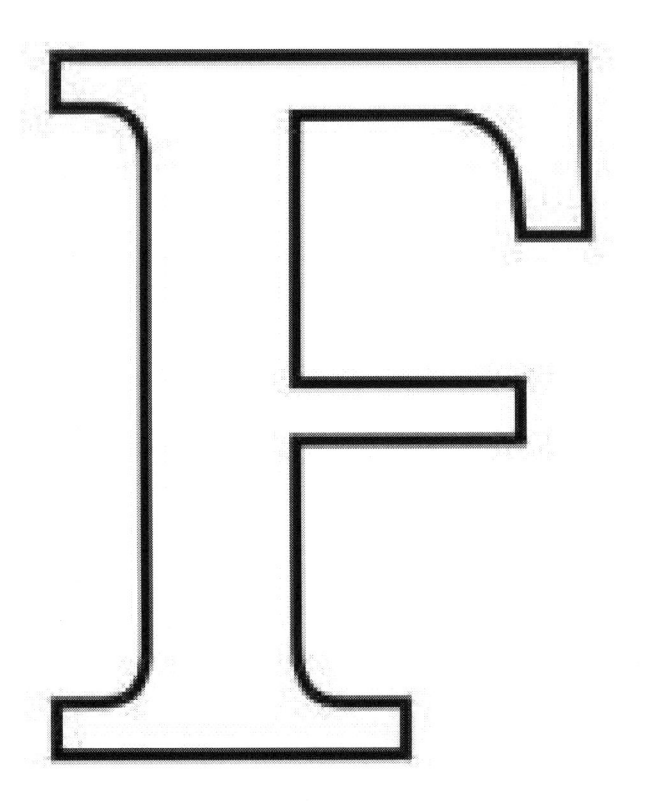

Feast day: November 24

St. Flora was born to a Christian mother and a Muslim father in Spain. She was secretly raised Catholic by her mother, but was betrayed by her brother and turned in to the Muslim judge. Her brother was told to beat her. She later met another wonderful Catholic named Mary. Together, they were again punished by a Muslim judge who sent them into an evil house to be abused by men. St. Eulogius, himself in prison, wrote them an encouraging letter, telling them that no matter what men may do to them, their souls belonged to God, as long as they remained faithful Catholics. They endured this suffering for years before they were finally beheaded. What a shining example she is to us!

St. Flora, pray for us!

F

G is for St. Gertrude the Great

Feast day: November 16

St. Gertrude was born in 1263. At the age of five, she went to a Benedictine abbey to be educated. She was a very good student, humble and obedient.

Because of her great devotion to Our Lord, she was blessed with special conversations with Our Lord and Mary. She was very gentle in her approach to everyone and especially devoted to the dear Holy Souls that are suffering in Purgatory. She taught us to release souls by praying, "Eternal Father, I offer Thee the most precious Blood of Thy Divine Son Jesus, in union with the Masses said throughout the world today, for all the Holy Souls in Purgatory. Amen."

St. Gertrude the Great, pray for us!

~15~

H is for St. Hubertus

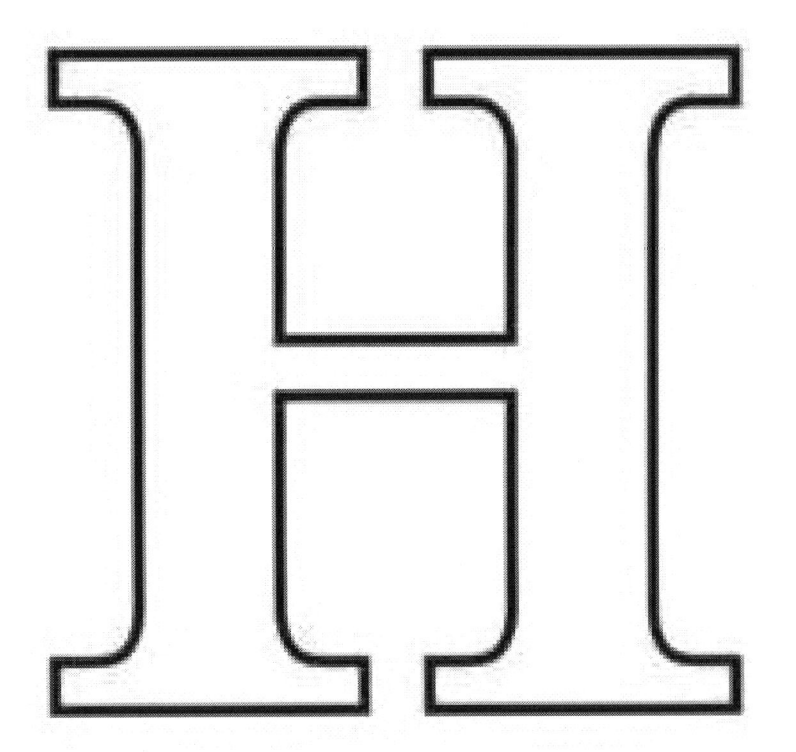

Feast day: November 3

Hubertus was an avid hunter who was entirely taken up with the affairs of the world. He did not care for our dear Catholic faith. One day, while he was hunting in the woods, he was chasing a great stag. When he came upon the majestic creature, he found it was beautifully white, and an image of Our Lord crucified was suspended in the air between its antlers. The vision made St. Hubertus understand that God is the only thing worth pursuing.

He was then ordained a priest and became a bishop. God also blessed him with the gift of miracles. He died in 727 while saying the Creed and the Our Father.

St. Hubertus, pray for us!

H

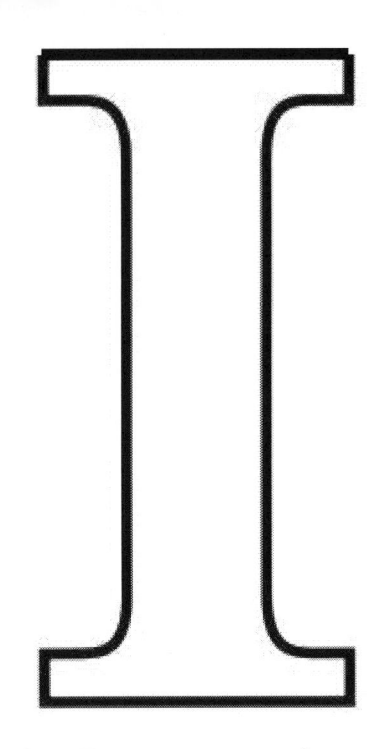

I is for St. Isaac Jogues

Feast day: September 26

St. Isaac was born in France in 1607. He devoted his life to the conversion of the Native Americans. He knew becoming a missionary to them would mean almost certain death, but sacrificed completely for God. He did much good and was also tortured several times by the Native Americans. He escaped America with his life, made his way back to France, and came before another priest who asked, "Do you know anything about Father Jogues?" Isaac replied, "He is not dead. He stands before you." Isaac held out his hands, which were missing fingers where the Native Americans had cut or bitten them off. The priest thanked God, "Dear God in Heaven!" and took Isaac into his arms! And yet, Isaac returned again to America by his own choice. He was killed with a hatchet by a Native American who later converted.

St. Isaac Jogues, pray for us!

I

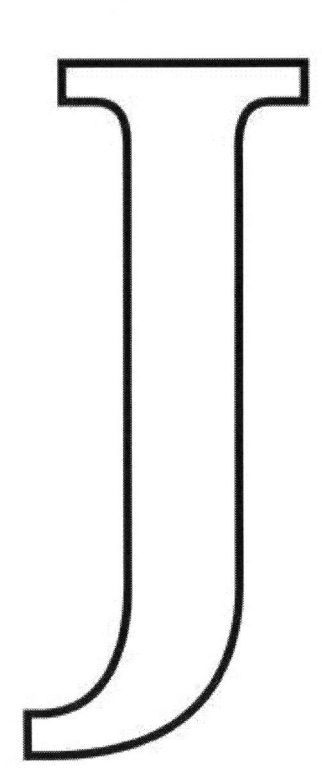

J is for St. Juliana Falconeri

Feast day: June 19

Juliana was born in 1270. She had a great sense of modesty and never even used a mirror or looked upon the face of a man as to guard her eyes carefully and avoid temptation. She received the habit from St. Philip Benizi. She was so humble and kind that she would work at healing the sick even by sucking with her own lips their ulcerous sores! While she was dying, she was visited by angels in the form of white doves and Jesus, as a Child, who crowned her with flowers. She could not take food at the end of her life which was a severe penance for her, especially not being able to receive Holy Communion. Her last day, she begged to adore Jesus. The Eucharist was laid upon her chest on a coporal. At that moment, she died, and the Eucharist disappeared, leaving the form stamped upon her heart for all to see.

St. Juliana Falconeri, pray for us!

~21~

K is for St. Kilian

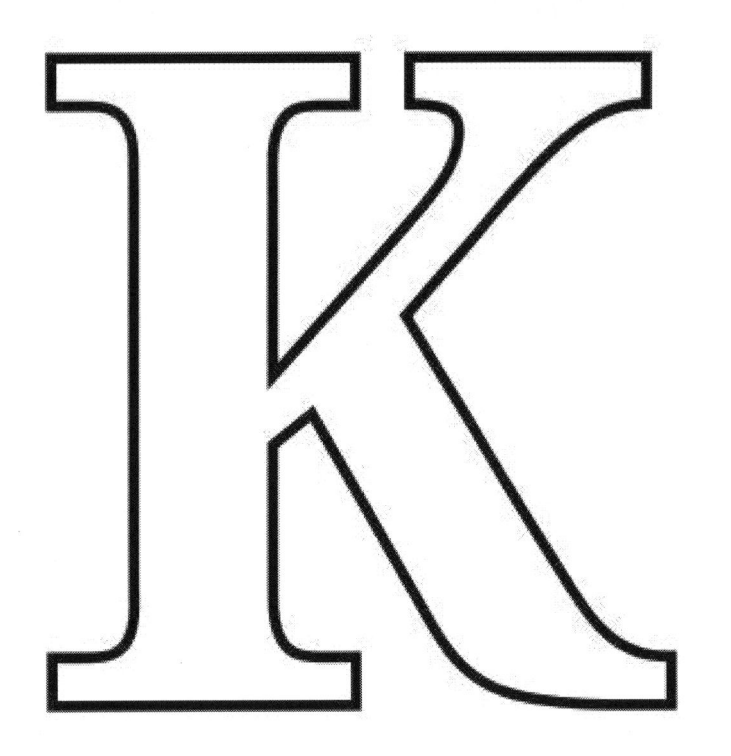

Feast day: July 8

Kilian was an Irish bishop who traveled to Germany to save souls. He came to the castle of Wurzburg where lived a pagan duke who was living in sin with a woman who was not his wife. Kilian was successful in helping the duke convert to the Catholic faith and then got the duke to understand that he must leave the woman living with him if he was to be in a state of grace. The woman was so angry that she had St. Kilian and his two companions murdered! She later went insane and died. The relics of St. Kilian have long produced miracles.

St. Kilian is a wonderful example to us in our present times where sins of impurity are so common and invalid unions are accepted, when they should be forbidden.

St. Kilian, pray for us!

K

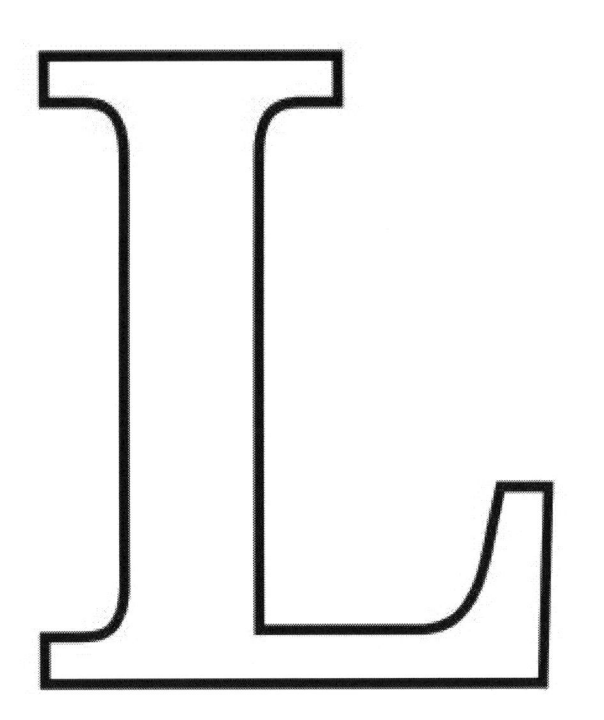

L is for St. Louis the King

Feast day: August 25

King Louis was a wonderful Catholic king of France. He became king at the age of just twelve and recited the Divine Office and heard two Masses every day! He branded people on the lips for sin of blasphemy and said he would gladly submit to it himself if it would mean no more blasphemy against our perfect God. The finest example of a Christian knight, he once was in his tent when a Muslim ruler ran inside. He held a bloody dagger as a threat to St. Louis, saying that he would kill him if he refused to make him a knight. Louis calmly answered that no unbeliever could ever perform the duties of a Catholic knight. Many times, Louis proved he would have rather given his life than cause God any pain through sin. He died by a brutal fever in 1270.

St. Louis, pray for us!

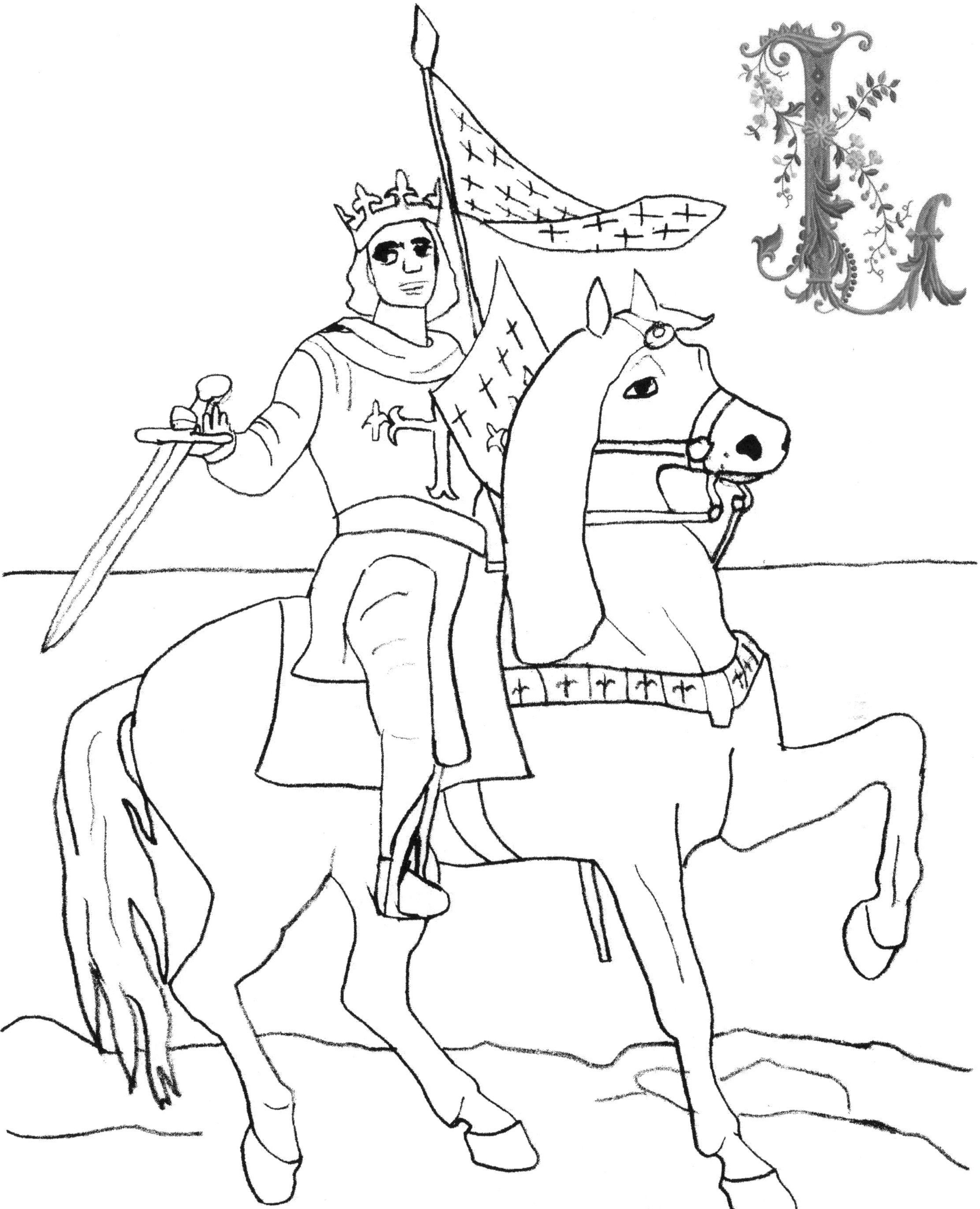
L

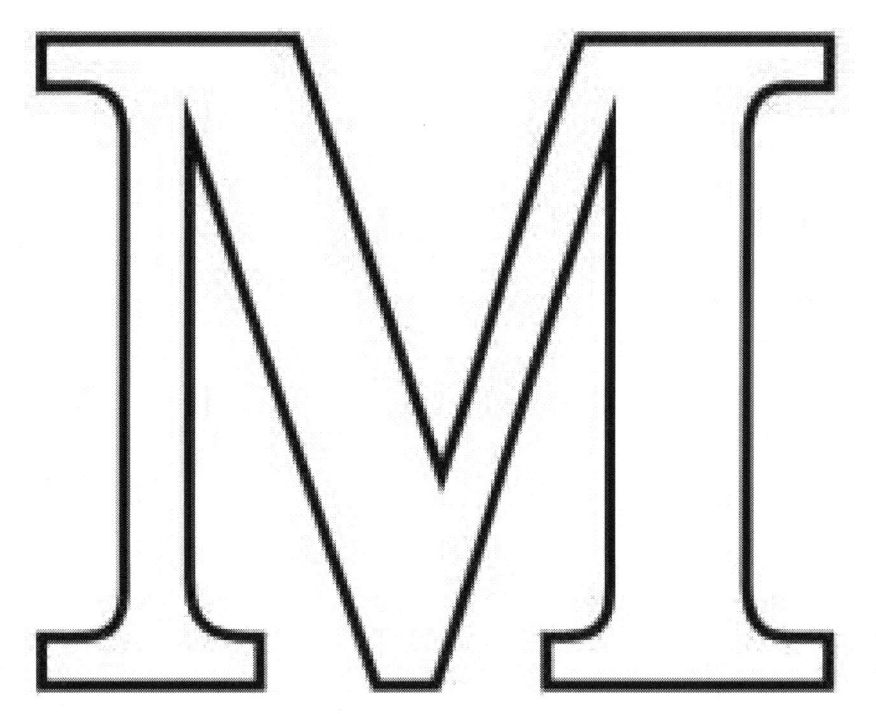

M is for St. Moses the Black

Feast day: August 28

Moses was born in 330 AD in Ethiopia. He led a life of evil, robbing and hurting people. One day, after committing a crime, he hid in a monastery. In doing so, he fell in love with the quiet, peaceful, and holy monks' way of life and their devotion to God. He then also became a monk.

Once he was attacked in his desert cell by robbers. He, being a strong and large man, overpowered all the intruders and dragged them to the other monks for advice on how to deal with them. The robbers then actually repented and became monks! Another time, when asked to judge a fellow monk, Moses came to the meeting with a leaking bag of sand. He said, "My sins run out behind me, and I do not see them, but today I am coming to judge the errors of another." The erring monk was then forgiven by all the monks.

St. Moses the Black, pray for us!

~27~

N is for St. Norbert

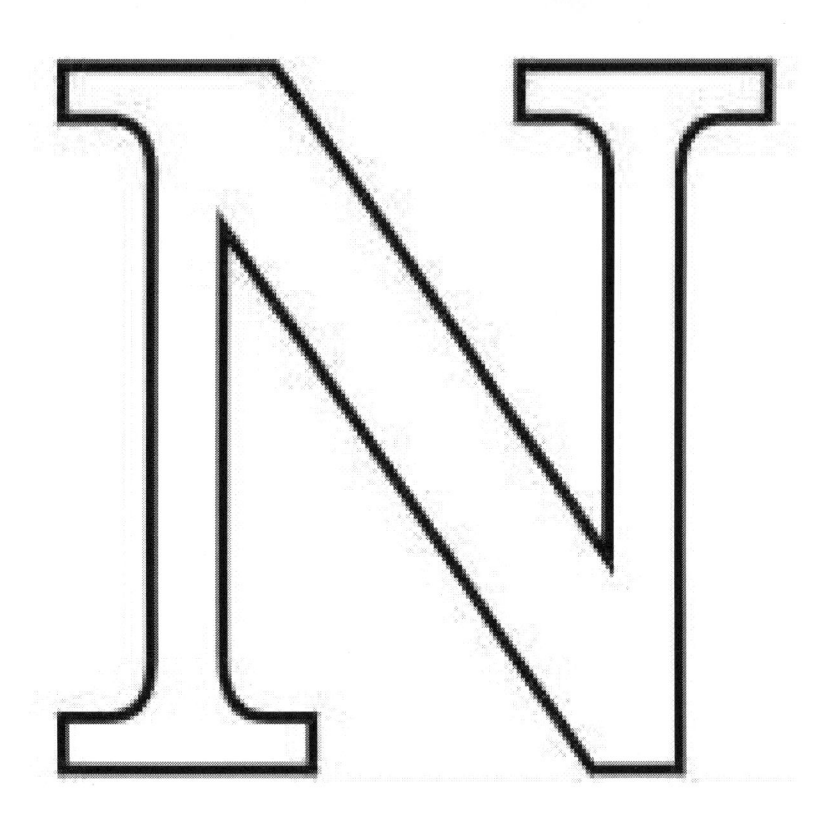

Feast day: June 6

Norbert was born in the 11th century. Once he was ordained a priest, he worked very hard for Our Lord. He was called upon to undo the damage that a heretic named Tankelin had done, mainly in denying the priesthood of the Catholic Church and blaspheming the Blessed Sacrament. St. Norbert renewed the faith of the people in this area, and told them to search for all the Sacred Hosts that the people had buried in filthy places to descrate Our Lord. The people found Them whole, and St. Norbert joyfully carried Them back to the tabernacle. He continued to spend his life in serving our beautiful Faith until he died at the age of fifty-three.

St. Norbert, pray for us!

~29~

O is for St. Olympias

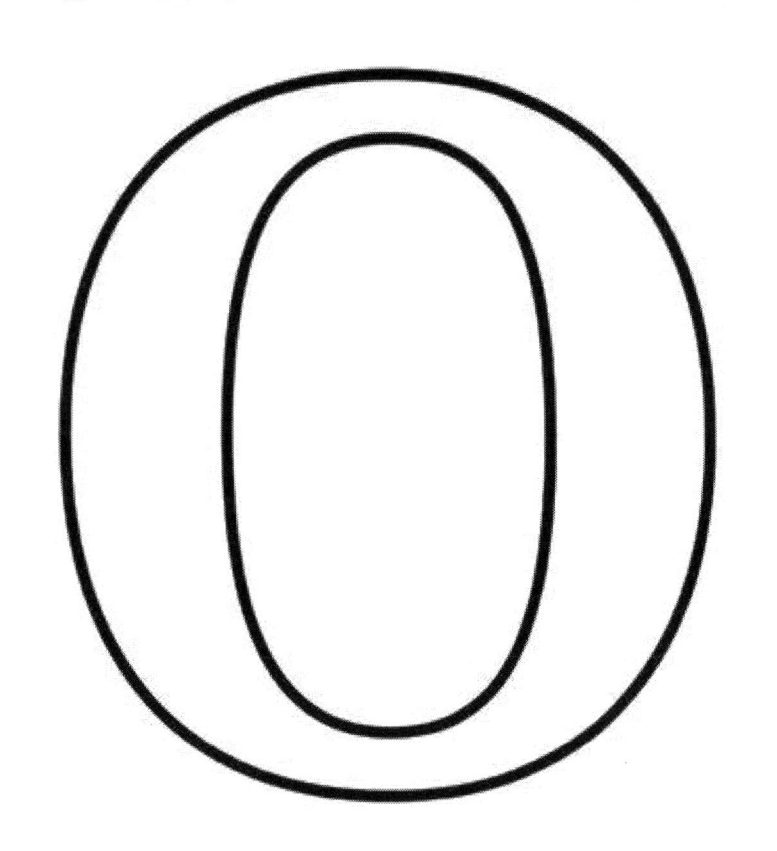

Feast day: December 17

St. Olympias was left an orphan at a very young age, but was raised by a pious Catholic whom she greatly resembled as a woman. Olympias married very young, but her husband died just twenty days after their wedding. She then decided never to marry again, but rather to serve Our Lord in everything. She gave her fortune to the poor and spent her time in prayer and works for the Church, such as preparing altar linens and other necessary duties. She was often accused falsely of many grievous things which she was innocent of, as well as other trials. A beautiful example of humility and obedience, St. Olympias died about 410 AD.

St. Olympias, pray for us!

~ 31 ~

P is for St. Philomena

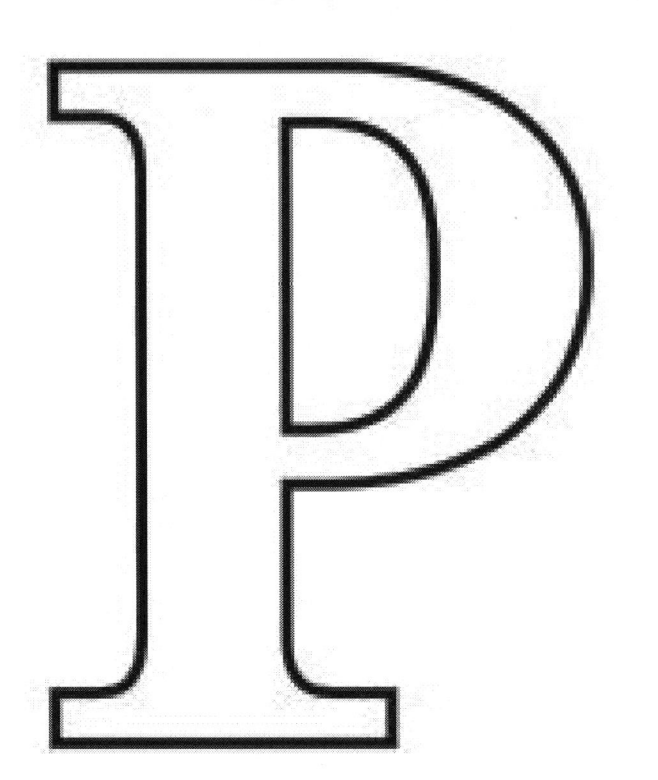

Feast day: August 11

St. Philomena, a princess, whose name means "Daughter of Light," consecrated herself to God when she was only eleven. Two years later, she was with her parents when they met with the Emperor Diocletian, who wanted desperately to marry her. She refused him, stating her dedication to God. Diocletian tried presents and then many horrible tortures to get Philomena to change her mind, but she never would. She was saved by an angel from being drowned in the river, the flaming arrows meant for her turned and killed the soldiers instead, and angels healed her wounds after the painful whippings. Finally, she died when pierced by a lance at the same hour Our Lord died on the cross.

St. Philomena, pray for us!

~ 33 ~

Q is for St. Quiteria

Feast day: May 22

St. Quiteria lived in Spain during the 5th century. It is said that she held two dogs with rabies at bay by the power of her sweet, saintly voice. She is therefore known as a patron to be invoked against rabies.

She died a virgin and a martyr for Our Lord. She was beheaded because she refused to marry and renounce our holy, Catholic faith. She much preferred the sweetness of a martyr's crown to one second's denial of our wonderful, loving Jesus Christ.

St. Quiteria, pray for us!

~35~

R is for St. Roch

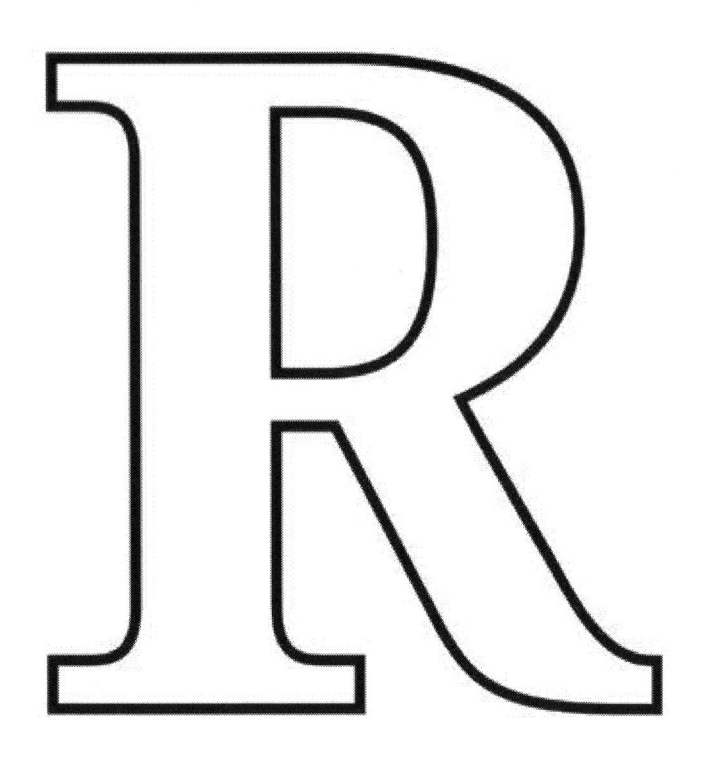

Feast day: August 16

St. Roch, also known as Roque, lived during the 14th century. Although a high noble, at the age of twenty, he gave all he had to the poor when his parents died. Many people at that time were sick with the plague, and he made it his life's work to help these sick as he could. In his work, he contracted the illness himself and found a lonely spot in the woods where Our Lord had a spring of water miraculously come up to nourish him. Our Lord also inspired the favorite dog of a nearby noble to bring him bread from his master's table every day to feed him! The owner eventually followed the dog out of curiosity, found Roch, and nursed him back to health. Roch miraculously cured many from the plague after this.

St. Roch, pray for us!

R

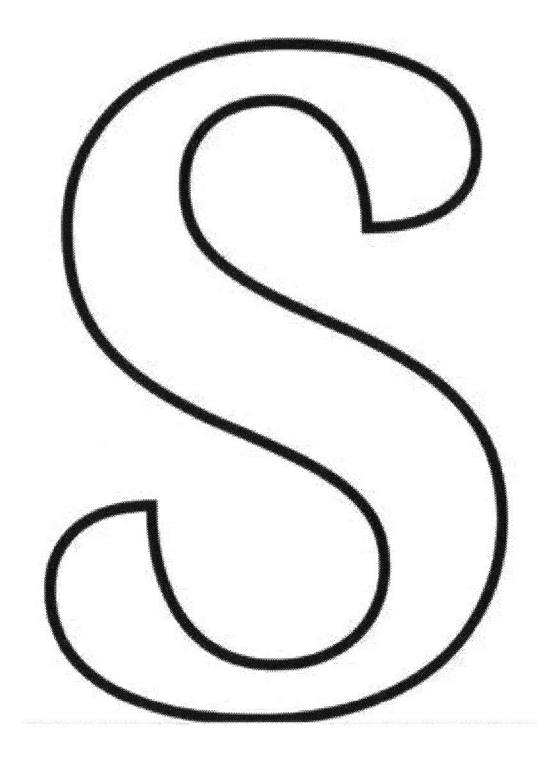

S is for St. Serenus

Feast day: February 23

When Serenus was young, he quit the world and bought a garden where he could live in purity, penance, and prayer. He lived on the fruits of his humble garden. Late one night, a woman came there with her two daughters. St. Serenus charitably corrected the woman to leave his garden as it was not appropriate for her to be there, especially so late at night. The woman took this as a personal offense and reported Serenus as insulting her grievously. The governor found Serenus to be innocent of any wrong, but in doing so, revealed that he was a Christian. St. Serenus happily submitted to his martyrdom saying, "I am ready to suffer all things for His Name!" He was immediately beheaded.

St. Serenus, pray for us!

~39~

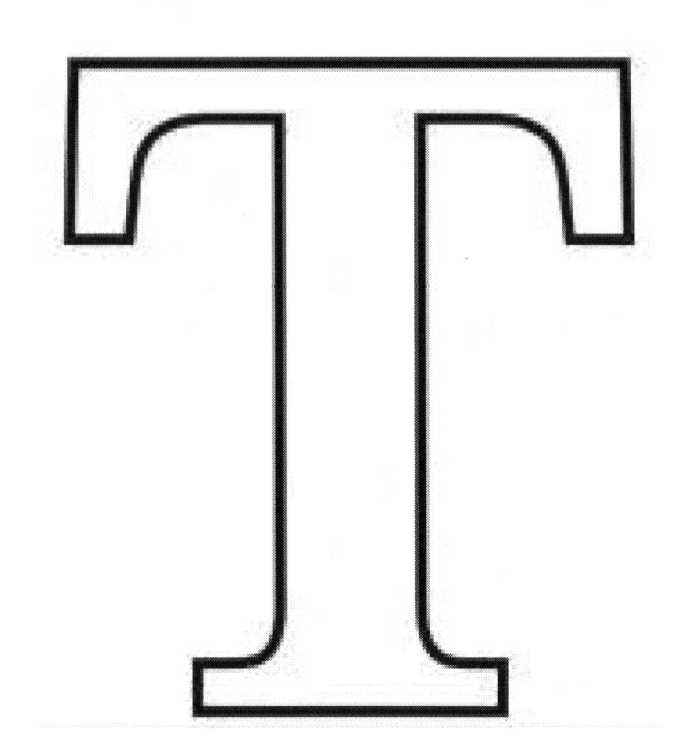

T is for St. Thomas More

Feast day: July 9

St. Thomas More was born in London, England in 1478. Because of his great intelligence, he quickly rose in nobility in the court of King Henry VIII and was made Lord Cancellor in 1529. He is a perfect example of putting God before human respect. King Henry VIII was furious because the pope would not grant him an annulment to his valid marriage. St. Thomas More was one of the few who defended the pope and the Catholic teaching on marriage. He refused to agree to the heresy that Henry VIII was the head of the Church in England. He refused to recognize the false marriage of Henry to a woman who was not his wife. For this, he was imprisoned and eventually beheaded.

St. Thomas More, pray for us!

T

U is for St. Ursula

Feast day: October 21

A Catholic teacher, Ursula had many young ladies under her care. She decided to travel to another land with her charges to hopefully be safe from the Saxons in her native England. When she and her companions arrived at Gaul, they were met by hordes of vicious Huns! St. Ursula and all her companions bravely resolved to meet death rather than do anything sinful whatsoever or deny God. They were all cruelly put to death by the Huns in the year 453.

St. Ursula is the patroness of teachers and young persons.

St. Ursula, pray for us!

~43~

V is for St. Victor

Feast day: July 21

St. Victor was a Catholic soldier who spent his nights visiting households to encourage them in the Faith during a time of great persecution from the Emperor Maximian. He, himself, was caught and told to deny Jesus. He refused and was then dragged through the city streets while being beaten by the people. Bruised and bleeding, he was then tortured on the rack until his tormenters were weak from exhaustion! Many more times he was tortured. Three days later, he was commanded to offer incense to a statue of Jupiter. Victor went up to the pagan altar and with one mighty kick, knocked down the statue and broke it! His leg was then cut off, and he was eventually beheaded. A true, strong hero!

St. Victor, pray for us!

V

W is for St. Winifred

Feast day: November 3

St. Winifred, also known as Winefride, was born in Wales, about the year 600. She was devout and consecrated herself to God as a young lady. Caradoc, the son of a prince, sought her hand in marriage. When he was refused by her, he became violent. Winifred ran away from him and when he caught up to her, in one swift blow, he cut her head off! It rolled down the hill where her uncle, St. Beuno, a priest, picked it up, carried it to her body, and then laid his cloak over. As he prayed for God's intercession, Caradoc was swallowed up by the earth and died! Winifred was then miraculously brought back to life! She became the abbess of a community of young maidens and lived a holy life.

St. Winifred, pray for us!

W

X is for St. Xystus

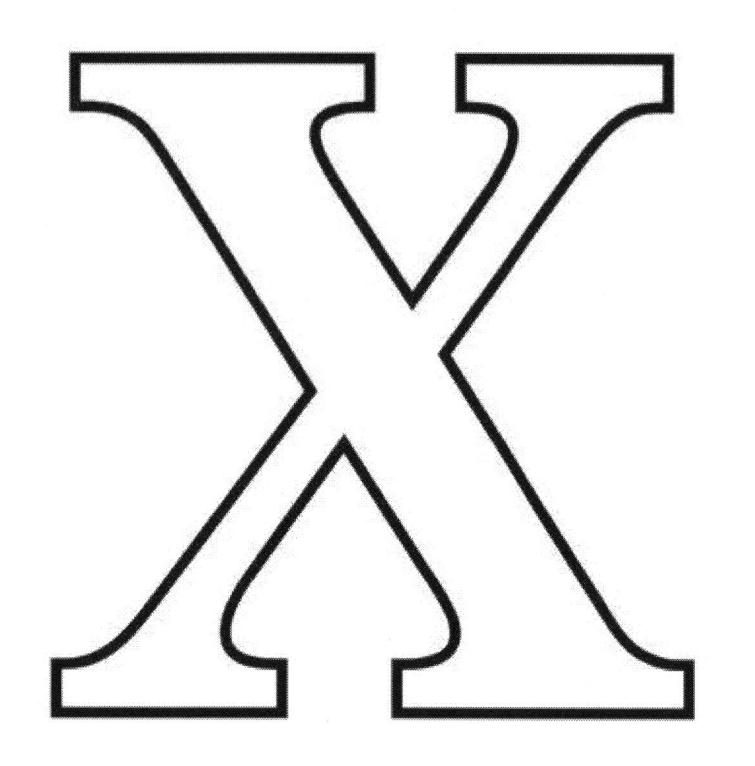

Feast day: August 6

Chosen to be pope in the year 257, St. Xystus was also known as Sixtus II. He was a strong defender against heresy. He was also forbidden to say Mass by those who were persecuting Catholics at the time, but continued to offer Mass regardless, as to honor Our Lord.

When he was caught, he was dragged out to be beheaded. On the way out, St. Lawrence cried, "I was your minister when you consecrated the Blood of Our Lord; Why do you leave me behind now that you are about to shed your own?" St. Xystus replied, "Do not weep, my son; in three days you will follow me." Indeed, this prophecy did come true! Let us remember what an honor it is to die for Christ!

St. Xystus, pray for us!

X

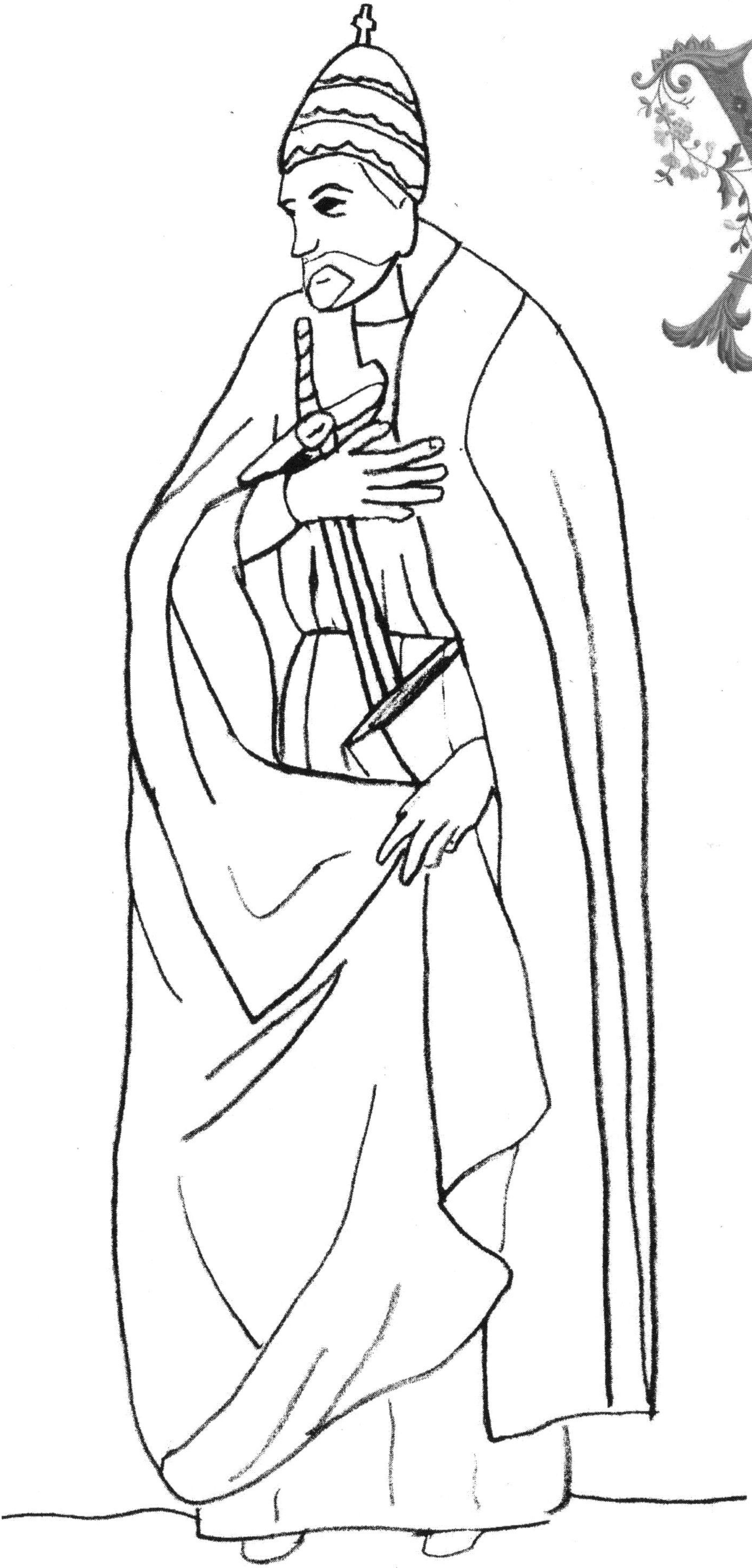

Y is for St. Yvo

Feast day: May 22

St. Yvo was born in 1258 to a noble family. As a young adult, he was ever striving towards holiness and made a vow of perpetual chastity despite the many marriage offers that were placed before him. He tirelessly worked to help the sick and the poor. He was ordained as a priest by his bishop who saw his great sanctity, even though he himself felt he was very unworthy of this honor.

He never delayed in doing good when it was able to be done. St. Yvo was a beautiful example of how we should offer sacrifices whenever we can, instead of putting off some great good we could do for someone now.

St. Yvo, pray for us!

~51~

Z is for St. Zita

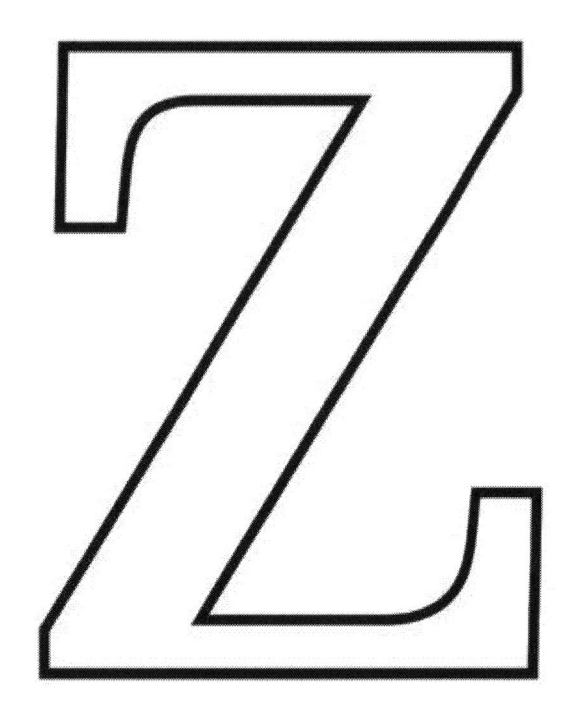

Feast day: April 27

St. Zita woke early each morning to go hear Mass, and then worked hard all day in the household of her master, for she was a servant. One day, when she was late in staying at Mass, she arrived home to find the bread already made. She assumed that one of the other servants had done this work for her. She thanked each one in turn, while they all told her that they had not made the bread. A wonderful smell came from the bread, and Zita knew that angels had made the bread while she had been praying at Mass! Zita ever remained gentle, even while the other servants would hit or yell at her out of jealousy and anger for her industrious and honest ways. She eventually converted the whole household through her lovely example!

She died in 1272.

St. Zita, pray for us!

~ 53 ~

Made in the USA
Columbia, SC
02 May 2022